SHARING GOD'S WORLD

ELIZABETH WHITE

Greek Orthodox Archdiocese of America
Department of Religious Education
Brookline, Massachusetts

Contents

UNIT **1** God Wants Us to Share

Lesson 1 WE BELIEVE
People Feel Happy When They Share

You're Invited TO A BIRTHDAY PARTY

HAPPY BIRTHDAY TO ANNA

Anna could not stop talking about her birthday party. "Mary is coming and George too," she said to her mother. "Irene doesn't know yet." Anna was excited and a little nervous. Would all her friends come?

Anna was not disappointed. Almost everyone came. She really liked the presents her friends brought. Just being together, talking, and laughing was great fun. Anna was happy to share this special day with people she loved. Later that evening she prayed, "Thank you God for this day, and thank you for my family and friends."

Some boys and girls think the best thing about a birthday party is receiving gifts. But what if you had gifts and no friends at your party? A party without friends would not be much fun. We enjoy talking, playing, and eating together. How do you feel when you plan your birthday party? What do you do to make it a special day? What is really important about birthday parties?

A Bible Story

Abraham Shares a Meal with Special Visitors

Abraham and Sarah lived in the land of **Canaan** many years before Jesus was born. On a hot summer day Abraham was sitting under an oak tree trying to keep cool. Suddenly he saw three men coming toward him. He knew that they were special visitors sent by God. They looked like angels. Abraham ran to meet them. He bowed to show his respect and said, "Please stay a while to rest, and have something to eat with us."

Then Abraham told his wife and servants, "Quick, let's bring some bread, milk, and meat for our guests." When everything was ready, Abraham served the food to his visitors.
As they were eating, the angels announced some wonderful news, "Sarah will give birth to a son in a year!" Abraham and Sarah were very old and had no children. The news made them very happy.

(Genesis 18: 1 - 15)

We call Abraham's kindness to the angels
"The Hospitality of Abraham." **Hospitality**
means sharing friendship and food with guests.
Abraham welcomed the angels and shared a
meal with them. Anna welcomed her friends
and shared the joy of her birthday with them.
We feel happy when we share with others.

The icon on this page is called
    "The Hospitality of Abraham."
Who are the people in this icon?

When we share we give a part of something that is ours to another person. We share food with guests. We share our toys when we play with friends.

We can also share our feelings and our thoughts when we talk with other people. We can share our talents by drawing a picture. Most important, we feel happy when we share love and friendship.

Activity A Sharing Tree

On each fruit write something you can share.

love

8

Lesson 2 WE BELIEVE
God Wants Us to Share

Try watching television with the sound turned off. This is what Andy's world is like. Andy is deaf. He has never heard people talk. His speech is hard to understand.

This does not stop Andy from sharing. He lets people know how he feels by using signs and by writing in a notebook or on a computer. His classmates enjoy his company because he is kind and smart. Right now he is teaching them sign language.

Andy had the best project in a science fair. He won first prize. The children in his class were happy for him. They shared in Andy's joy, except Ed. He was jealous. Ed could only think of himself. He could not share in Andy's joy.

Science Fair

A Bible Story

Cain and Abel Bring Gifts to God

Adam and Eve's first two sons were called Cain and Abel. Cain was a farmer. Abel was a shepherd. Cain was very selfish. When he did not get his way, he became jealous and angry. Abel loved God. He was a good and honest man.

There came a time when Cain and Abel brought gifts to God. Cain offered wheat from his fields, and Abel offered a lamb from his flock. God was pleased with Abel's gift, but not with Cain's. That made Cain very angry!

God said to Cain, "Why are you angry?
You must turn away from sin, from thinking
wrong thoughts and doing wrong things.
Then, you will not be angry and you will be
able to give with a good heart."

Cain did not listen to God. Instead he turned
his anger toward his brother and killed him in
the fields. Later, God asked Cain, "Where is
your brother?" Cain answered, "I don't know!
Am I supposed to take care of my brother?"
Cain did not want to say he had done
something terribly wrong. He was not even
sorry for it. God punished Cain by sending
him to a faraway land.

(Genesis 4: 1 - 16)

11

We do not offer lambs or bundles of wheat today but we do share many things with God. We can offer Him many gifts. We can bake the prosforo, go to church, sing the hymns, and pray at home. We can give food or money to the poor.

All these gifts are good. But we should offer them with love and kindness. When we sin, it is hard to give with love and kindness. When that happens we must think about what we have done or said. Then we should say, "I'm sorry." This way, goodness can fill our hearts again, and we can share with joy. The Bible says, "I may give away everything I have but if I have no love, this does me no good."

Lesson 3 WE BELIEVE
We Share in Abraham's Blessing

Tim remembers how he liked serving in the altar when he was a little boy. He loved being in God's house and hearing about what Jesus said and did.

As he was growing up Tim thought that he might want to become a math teacher like his father. But he was not sure. There was something in his heart telling him that he really wanted to be a priest. Was it God telling him?

Now many years later, Tim knows that God wants him to become a priest. He is going to a school called a **seminary**. He feels blessed and his heart is filled with joy. Tim is glad to have obeyed God's call.

A Bible Story

God Calls Abraham

Let's say Abraham kept a diary.
This is what it might say.

My home is a tent in the desert. The people in my family keep their tents near mine. We move around a lot, looking for food and water for the animals. I own many goats, camels, and sheep. But all my riches cannot buy the one thing my wife Sarah and I want most, a child.

God spoke to me today. He said, "Go. Leave your father's family. Go to a new land, the land of Canaan, which I will give you and your children. You will be the father of a great nation." I do not understand what God means. But my faith is strong. I will listen to God and obey. Tomorrow, Sarah and I will leave with my nephew and all my servants. We will go where God wants us to go.

~·~

How God has blessed me! Some years ago, God sent angels to visit me. Sarah and I have a son now. His name is Isaac. I have a new land which is rich in crops. God has promised that I will have many grandchildren and many more great-grandchildren. He said, "They will be as many as the stars in the sky." Now I understand what God told me long ago. Thank you God for all your blessings.

The promise that God made to Abraham is called a **covenant**. A covenant is when two people make promises to each other. God made a promise to Abraham and Abraham promised to obey God. This is how Abraham became the father of the Hebrew people.

Jesus was born among the Hebrew people many years later. All those who follow Jesus are called Christians. They are the people of the Church. Through Jesus we are all God's people. We share in Abraham's blessings. Like Abraham, we should have strong faith in God. We should love and obey God all the time.

God has plans for everyone. God has a plan for you. What do you want to be when you grow up? You may not know yet. Be ready to listen to what God tells you in your heart.

Activity Circle every second letter to find out what God has called us all to do. Write your answer on the lines.

A B C E F L H I P E S V X

E V I P N R G J O K D H

_____

_____

_____

_____

Lesson 4 WE BELIEVE
We Share God's Gift to Moses

Georgia had just finished putting her toys away. "Now, can I watch TV, Mom?" "Now it's time to get ready for bed," said her mother. "Oh, all right," answered Georgia. She was brushing her teeth when she thought, "I wish I didn't have to follow any rules."

That night Georgia had a dream. She dreamt that she did not ever have to go to school. She had chocolate ice cream for breakfast every morning. She could watch TV as long as she wanted.

Have you ever had a dream like that? What would happen to Georgia if her dream came true?

Color in red what is wrong in the picture.

God's Law

The Hebrews had a great leader named Moses. Remember, Moses led them out of Egypt to go to the Promised Land.

On their way during that long trip, the people camped at **Mount Sinai**. God told Moses to climb the mountain. There, God gave Moses the Ten Commandments and other rules. We call all these laws **God's Law**.

Many years after the time of Moses, Jesus taught His followers how to obey God's Law. He said, "I have not come to do away with the Law, but to make its teachings come true."

All Christians share God's gift of the Law to Moses. Jesus said that of all the laws, two are the most important, "The greatest commandment is, 'You shall love the Lord your God with all your heart, and with all your soul, and with all your mind, and with all your strength.' The second greatest is this, 'You shall love your neighbor as yourself.' There are no other commandments greater than these."

   We need rules to live together with other
people. We follow rules at home, at church,
and at school. We obey the laws of our country.
Above all, we must obey God's laws and follow
the teachings of Jesus.

   Loving God means putting Him first in our
lives. We show our love for God when we go to
church, when we receive Holy Communion, and
when we pray. Loving our neighbor as
ourselves means that we care about other
people the way we care about ourselves.
When we love and respect one another, we
show that we love God and obey His Law.

22

Activity   Write Right or Wrong after the following statements:

1. Your friend Nicholas says that fasting is not an important rule. So, you decide not to fast before Holy Communion.

   _____

2. Your friend has a hard time with math. You spend some time helping him.

   _____

3. Your ball rolls out into a busy street. You chase after it without looking.

   _____

4. There is a new boy in the class. You ask him to play with your friends after school.

   _____

Lesson 5 WE BELIEVE
God's People Give Thanks

Helen was excited about the new school year. She liked her teacher. It was good to see all her friends again. Helen had a new school bag, a new notebook binder, and new sneakers.

But Helen's parents could not afford to buy her new clothes that year. Her older cousin Vicky gave her a coat and some pants she had outgrown. They were like new. Helen was happy to have them.

Next time Helen saw her cousin she said,
"Vicky, I loved the clothes you gave me. Look!
They're just my size. Thank you so much."
That made Vicky feel good. "I am glad you like
them," she said. From then on the two shared
many things.

A Bible Story

The Hebrews Build the Tabernacle

God freed the Hebrews from the land of Egypt where they were slaves. On their way to the Promised Land, He protected them from enemies. God gave them food and water. He gave them His Law to help them live together.

The Hebrew people were happy to receive God's gifts. But sometimes they forgot to thank Him. Instead they complained about the long journey and the hard life in the desert. So, God asked Moses and the people to build a special tent where they could come to pray to Him. It was called a **tabernacle**.

Everyone was excited about building God's tent. People brought gifts of gold, linen, and wool. The men made poles to hold up the tent and make it easy to carry. When the tabernacle was finished all the people came together to give thanks to God. They were glad to have a place where they could pray to Him. Now they could remember to thank God always.

(Exodus 35 - 36)

As Orthodox Christians we believe that we should give thanks for what we have and what we share. First, remember to give thanks to God. Before meals, thank God for your food. At bedtime, thank Him for the day. When you go to church, thank Him for all His gifts. When your father or mother helps you figure out your homework, give them a hug and say "thank you." When you receive a gift, send a thank you card. When anyone helps you, always say "thank you." Giving thanks is an important part of sharing.

Do you remember to give thanks? Think of all the things you share with God, with your family, and with others. What are they?

Here are some prayers you can say to give thanks to God. Remember to make the Sign of the Cross when you pray.

A morning prayer

Lord, thank you for the gift of this new day.
Give me the courage to be honest, kind, and
helpful to others.
Fill my heart with love and joy.
Amen.

An evening prayer

Lord, thank you for all the good things of this day.
Bless my family, my teachers, and all those who love
me and care for me.
Forgive me for any wrong things that I may have
said or done.
Give peace to the world.
Bless me that I may sleep in peace.
Amen.

UNIT 1 Review

New Words I Have Learned About

Canaan   hospitality   seminary
covenant   Mount Sinai   God's Law
tabernacle

We Believe

People Feel Happy When They Share
God Wants Us to Share
We Share in Abraham's Blessing
We Share God's Gift to Moses
God's People Give Thanks

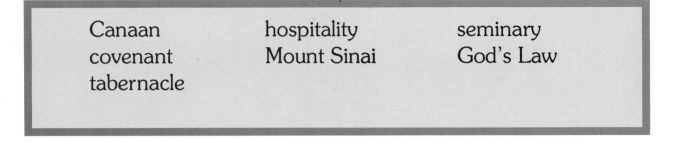

Check-up

Unscramble the words below. Then, choose the
correct word to complete each sentence.

tyalhpisiot   acetnnov   alcbaterne
aaannC   ariesmny

1. Abraham and Sarah lived in _____ when the angels visited them.

_____

2. _____ means sharing a meal with guests.

_____

3. Tim went to the _____ to study how to be a priest.

_____

4. God had a _____ with Abraham.

_____

5. The _____ was a place where the Hebrews prayed to God.

_____

UNIT 2 Jesus Teaches Us to Share

33

Lesson 1 WE BELIEVE
Jesus Brings Us the Good News

What a happy day! Amy had a big smile on her face. She rushed through the door of St. Luke's Hospital. Her father was right behind her, holding a red rose.

"May I help you?" asked the woman behind the desk. "We're here to take my new baby brother home!" announced Amy. "Oh, what wonderful news," said the woman.

Amy and her father hurried to Mom's room. There was her mother holding little Michael. Almost out of breath, Amy said, "He's so small! Can I hold him, please, Mom?"

When they arrived home, they saw Amy's older brother waving from the porch. He was holding a big sign that said, "It's a boy!"

Their friends across the street came out to greet the mother and the new baby. Soon, everyone in the neighborhood was happy to hear the good news.

When you hear good news, what do you do? What good news have you heard this week?

A Bible Story

Jesus Announces the Good News

By the time of Jesus, the Hebrew people were called Jews. They prayed in places called **synagogues**. Jesus often went to synagogues to pray and teach.

Once, Jesus went to the synagogue in Nazareth, the town where He grew up. The synagogue was full. All eyes were fixed on Jesus. He took a Bible and he read this part:

"The Spirit of God is on me.
He has chosen me to bring you good news.
He has sent me to free people from their
sins and to cure the sick.
I am here to tell you that the time has now
come for God to save His people."

When Jesus finished reading, He said, "These words are about me. I am the one God sent to share the good news of His love. I am the Savior." The people could not believe what Jesus said. He was only a carpenter's son. They had known Him since He was a little boy. How could he claim to do things that only God could do?

(Luke 4: 14 - 22)

37

Christians believe Jesus is the Savior. He is the most important part of the good news. Do you remember what the angel announced to the shepherds when Jesus was born? The angel said, "I am here with good news for you, which will bring great joy to the world. On this day your Savior was born."

Jesus is also called **Christ**. This word means the greatest leader chosen by God to save the world.

I AM THE LIGHT OF THE WORLD HE THAT FOLLOWETH ME, SHALL NOT WALK IN DARKNESS, BUT SHALL HAVE THE LIGHT OF LIFE.

Christ brought the good news that God loves us so much that He forgives our sins when we are truly sorry. Christ taught that we should love and forgive one another. When we believe in Jesus and show love and forgiveness we live God's way. This is the good news that we should share with all people.

Lesson 2 WE BELIEVE
Jesus Calls Us to Be His Helpers

New books had arrived for the third grade. "I need some volunteers to bring them from the office," Mr. Franklin said. Every hand in the class went up.

"I think the office would get a little crowded with all of you there," the teacher laughed. "Three should be enough to do the job. But I'm glad so many of you want to help. Greg, Eric, and Maria, go to the office and bring the books here."

At school you can help in many ways. Teachers like to have help in the classroom. It makes their job easier. How do you help your teacher?

A Bible Story

The First Disciples

One day Christ was walking along the shore of the **Sea of Galilee**. He saw two boats on the beach. Four fishermen were washing their nets. Jesus got into one of the boats. It belonged to Peter and his brother Andrew. "Push your boat out in deep water and let down your nets," Jesus told Peter.

Peter said, "Master, we worked hard all night and we caught nothing. But I will do as you say." Then an amazing thing happened. They caught so many fish that their nets were breaking! They waved to the other two fishermen to come and help them. John and James came out on their boat. Soon both boats were full of fish.

Peter knew he was seeing a miracle. He fell on his knees before Jesus and said, "Go away from me Lord, because I am a sinful man."

"Don't be afraid," Jesus answered, "from now on you will be **fishers of people**."

Peter, Andrew, James, and John pulled their boats up on the beach. Then they left everything and followed Jesus. They became His first disciples.

(Luke 5: 1 - 11)

When Christ said to Peter and the other fishermen, "you will be fishers of people," He meant that they would be His helpers. Instead of catching fish, they would now teach people to live God's way. They would help Jesus to bring the good news of God's love to all people.

Jesus wants all of us to be His disciples. Boys and girls often think they are too young to help Jesus. That is not true.

- Can you cheer up someone who is sad?
- Can you help your teacher at school?
- Can you invite a friend to church?
- Can you pray for others?
- Yes! You can.

You can be a good disciple. You can help Jesus bring the good news to others.

Lesson 3 WE BELIEVE
Jesus Shows Us How to Share

"Look at that one! It would make a great jack-o-lantern," said Dan to Alex. Dan's class was on a field trip at a pumpkin farm. Everyone was enjoying the fresh air and looking at all the pumpkins.

Later, they stopped at a park to eat. Everyone had brought their lunch. Everyone, that is, except Josh. "Oh no! I forgot mine!" he said, "It's at school."

"That's okay," said Dan, "you can have some of my sandwich".

Beth asked, "Would you like some potato chips too? Come and sit with us!"

Why did Dan and Beth share their lunch with Josh? Explain how Josh felt.

43

A Bible Story

Jesus Feeds 5000 People

A boy was walking to his village. He was carrying a basket with five loaves of bread and two fish. On the way he saw many people on a hillside gathered around Jesus. The boy squeezed through the crowd to get near Him. Then he listened to every word Jesus said.

At the end of the day, everyone was hungry. Jesus asked His disciples, "How can we feed so many people?" Andrew answered, "Here is a boy with five loaves and two fish. But these are not enough for everybody." The boy heard Andrew and ran up to Jesus saying, "Please take my loaves and fish. We can all share them."

Jesus was pleased with the boy's gift. He said a prayer and blessed the five loaves and two fish. There were now many loaves and many fish. Jesus gave them to His disciples and the disciples gave them to the people. Everyone ate as much as they wanted, and there was still some food left. Jesus said, "Gather the pieces left over. Let us not waste anything." The crowd was amazed at the miracle.

(John 6: 1-14)

45

No one likes going hungry. We need food to
live. We pray to God, "Give us this day our
daily bread." God wants us to share our food
with those who are hungry.

To remember this, Orthodox Christians have
a special service called the Blessing of the Five
Loaves. Five loaves of bread are placed on a
small table in church.

The priest offers prayers thanking God for His gifts. We also pray for peace in the world. Then the loaves are cut in small pieces and shared by everyone.

This service reminds us of how Jesus blessed the five loaves and fed many people. It helps us remember to thank God for His love and His gifts. We know that when God's love is in our hearts, we want to share what we have with others. When we share, we show that God's love is in us.

At the end of the Blessing of the Five Loaves, we sing,

"Rich people have become poor and hungry, but those who seek the Lord will never go without a blessing."

Look through some magazines and find a picture of poor people . Cut it out and tape it in the box below. Then write what you can do to help those people.

Lesson 4 WE BELIEVE
Jesus Asks Us to Carry the Cross

When Jason Gaes was six years old he was told that he had cancer. His family was very upset. He was scared. He did not know what was going to happen to him. Jason spent a lot of time in the hospital. Later he became well again.

Jason thought about other children who get cancer. He wanted to give them hope. When he was eight years old he wrote a book called, "My Book For Kids With Cansur." It tells them what to expect when they have to be in the hospital.

This difficult experience taught Jason many things. He learned a lot about doctors and hospitals. Most of all, he learned how it feels to be very sick. He decided to use that knowledge to help others. Now Jason wants to become a doctor so he can keep on helping sick children.

A Bible Story

Jesus Is Crucified

When Christ finished The Last Supper with His disciples, He went to a garden to pray. The disciples followed Him. While they were in the garden, soldiers came and arrested Jesus. The disciples ran away because they were afraid.

The soldiers took Jesus to the leaders of the Jewish people. One of the leaders asked Jesus, "Are you the Son of God?" Jesus said, "Yes. I am." The leaders did not believe Him. They became very angry at Jesus for saying such a thing. They decided that Jesus should be crucified.

So, they took Jesus to **Pontius Pilate**, the Roman **governor**. Pontius Pilate asked Jesus many questions. Then he turned to the leaders and said, "What crime has Jesus done? He does not deserve to die." But the leaders and a crowd with them began to shout, "Crucify Him!" Pilate was not able to change their minds. He told the soldiers to take Jesus and crucify Him.

50

As the soldiers took Jesus away, they made Him carry the cross. The cross was heavy and Jesus fell. The soldiers forced another man to carry the cross to a place called **Golgotha**. There, they crucified Jesus and two other prisoners. While Jesus was on the cross, He said, "Father, forgive them, for they do not know what they are doing."

(Mark 14:32 - 15:24 and Luke 22:14 - 22:34)

Jesus suffered for doing the work that God sent Him to do. Jesus came to tell us that He was the Son of God. He brought us a message of love from God. He taught us to love and forgive one another.

He also taught us that these things are hard to do. It is hard to be kind to someone who is unfair to you. It is even harder to be good to others when you are sick or hurt. This is why Jesus taught, "If anyone wants to come with me, he must forget himself, carry his cross, and follow me."

To do something hard is like carrying a heavy load. It can be called carrying a cross. How can you be a true follower of Christ? By doing good always and by thinking of others more than about yourself. Instead of playing with your best friend, you might go with your parents to visit someone who is sick. Instead of buying another baseball glove, you can give the money to help poor people. Sometimes helping others means giving up what you really want for yourself.

This is what it means to carry the cross.

What happened to Jason that was like carrying a cross? Tell about a time when you had to do something hard. What does Jesus teach us about carrying a cross?

UNIT 2 Review

New Words I Have Learned About

synagogues   Christ   Sea of Galilee
fishers of people   Pontius Pilate   governor
Golgotha

We Believe

Jesus Brings Us the Good News
Jesus Calls Us to Be His Helpers
Jesus Shows Us How to Share
Jesus Asks Us to Carry the Cross

Check Up

Write a letter to a friend. Tell him or her what you know about Jesus. Remember to tell your friend what Jesus teaches us.

Dear ————————

————————————————————

————————————————————

————————————————————

————————————————————

————————————————————

————————————————————

————————————————————

————————————————————

————————————————————

————————————————————

———————————————————— (your name)

UNIT 3 The Holy Spirit Helps Us to Share

Lesson 1 WE BELIEVE
The Holy Spirit
Helps Us to Work Together

Janet has just come home from a softball game. "How did your team do?" asked her father. "Oh, we lost," replied Janet. "But it was a close game. Everybody played hard. We made some good catches. The coach said that if we keep up our teamwork we will win our share of games."

"I think that's right," said Janet's father. "Teamwork is very important. The players should help each other. It sounds like you have a good coach."

Have you ever been on a team? How did you feel about playing together?

A Bible Story

The Day of Pentecost

Fifty days after the resurrection of Jesus, the disciples met together to pray. Suddenly they heard a noise in the room like a rushing wind. Small flames of fire appeared above each person. The disciples were filled with the Holy Spirit. We call this event **Pentecost**. Pentecost means the fiftieth day after the resurrection of Jesus.

On that day the disciples received God's power to bring the good news about Jesus to all people. From that day they were called **Apostles**. An Apostle is a person who is sent out to share the good news.

After the Apostles received the Holy Spirit, they went out and talked to a large crowd of people about Jesus. Many believed the good news. Three thousand were baptized. They were the first Christians.

The Apostles and the first Christians were full of excitement. The Holy Spirit filled their hearts with love and goodness. They met every day to have a meal and to pray. They loved one another so much they shared everything they had. They sold things they owned and gave the money to the Apostles. Then, the Apostles gave it to the poor. As people heard the good news about Jesus and saw the love of Christians, many more joined the Church.

(Acts of the Apostles chapters 2 and 4)

61

We received the Holy Spirit at our baptism.
When the Holy Spirit fills our hearts with love,
there is no room for unkindness and selfishness.
Christians are like a team working together.
The Holy Spirit helps us to love one another
and to share what we have. God gives us the
Holy Spirit to keep us united in love
and goodness.

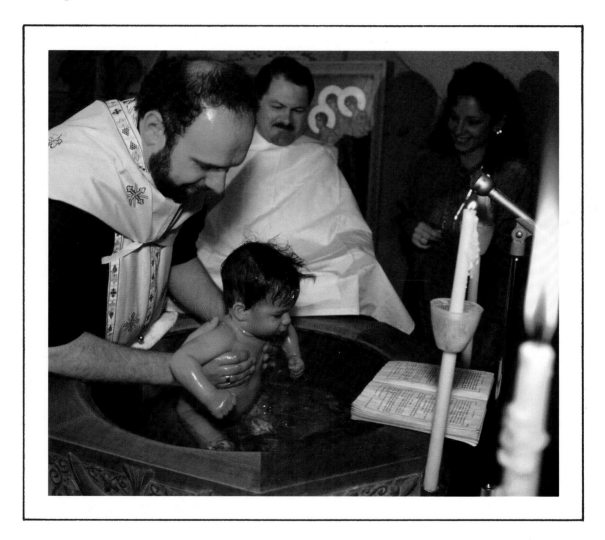

Why is teamwork important?
How do Christians work together?

Think of a team that you belong to.
Write one thing on each player's shirt that you
think would help a team work together.

Lesson 2 WE BELIEVE
The Holy Spirit Helps Us to Share the Good News

"Is my face red?" Nick wondered to himself. "Everyone is looking at me. I wish I could sit down."

It was Nick's turn to give a talk to his Church school class. He had done a lot of work on it but he was nervous. Nick took a deep breath and began.

Somehow he found the courage to do it. The class listened to him. When he finished Nick sat down. Mrs. Michaels said, "Very good!"

Have you ever given a talk? Tell the class about it.

The judges ordered Peter and John to stop talking about Jesus. The Apostles told them, "We must obey God. We have to keep on talking about what Jesus said and did."

The judges did not know what to do. How could they say that the miracle had not happened? Everyone in Jerusalem had heard that the crippled man could now walk. So, they let Peter and John go.

(Acts of the Apostles 3:1 - 4:22)

Have you ever felt scared? Have your friends ever turned against you? Sometimes life can be difficult. When we have problems we can ask the Holy Spirit to guide us.

Remember to pray every day and ask for God's strength. The Holy Spirit will help you to say and to do the right things. Your good example is the best way you can share the good news with others.

Lesson 3 WE BELIEVE
The Holy Spirit Gives Us Courage

"Let's get even with Rick," said Todd, "by letting the air out of his bicycle tires."

"We could put a hole in his soccer ball," added Tony.

"No, I have a better idea," laughed John, "Let's break Mrs. Hagen's window with his softball and blame it on him!"

But Bill was silent. Finally he got up enough courage to speak out. "Let's not do anything. It's wrong. I won't do it."

His friends looked at him. They began laughing and teasing. "What's the matter? Are you afraid?"

They walked away from him. But they kept thinking about what Bill had said. After a while, they gave up their plans to play a mean trick.

The Story of a Saint

St. Stephen the First Martyr

The Apostles were the leaders of the first Christians. They chose seven helpers called deacons. One of the deacons was named **Stephen**. He was filled with the Holy Spirit and he was strong in his faith.

One day Stephen was arrested for talking about Jesus. He was taken before the court. There he reminded the judges of how God sent Abraham and Moses to help the Hebrew people. "Now," said Stephen, "God sent Jesus, and you killed Him."

70

The judges became very angry. Then Stephen looked and said, "I see heaven and Jesus next to God!" The judges and the people flew into a rage. They dragged Stephen out and threw heavy stones at him. Before Stephen died, he prayed, "Lord, forgive them."

St. Stephen was the first **martyr** of the Church. A martyr is a saint who dies for his faith.

The Holy Spirit gave St. Stephen the courage to stand up for what he believed. He was filled with the Holy Spirit because his faith was strong. God gave him the power he needed.

We must not be afraid to stand up for what we believe. We must do the right thing, even if others are doing wrong. What did Bill do when his friends wanted to play a trick? What does the word courage mean to you? Do you know some people who have shown courage?

Activity Complete each story
with an ending that shows courage.

Before Mrs. Wilson left the classroom she asked the class to work on their assignment. After she left, some people started running around the room.

_____

_____

_____

_____

_____

Peter was practicing for the soccer tryouts. His friends said that he would never make the team. "Maybe I shouldn't try out after all," Peter said to himself.

_____

_____

_____

_____

_____

_____

Lesson 4 WE BELIEVE
The Holy Spirit
Helps Us to Love Others

Katy stood by her front window and watched the new family move in next door. She recognized the girl carrying a box into the house. "Oh, not her!" she said. "That's Mary. She's in my class at school. Nobody likes her."

"Why?" asked Katy's brother.

"She never talks to people," Katy answered, "and she's so weird. At lunch she sits by herself. She never joins anything."

"Come on! Has she done anything to you?" asked her brother. "Give her a chance."

Katy tried to make friends with Mary.
She invited Mary over to watch a video.
They rode their bikes together. Then, one day
Mary brought Katy a gift. "I painted this myself,"
she said. "It's a picture of you and me.
I want you to have it. You are my first real friend."

That night Katy said to her brother, "Mary is
so talented. And she talks a lot once you get to
know her. I really like Mary."

A Bible Story

An Enemy Becomes a Friend

Saul was an enemy of the first Christians. He had permission to arrest them. He looked for ways to destroy the Church. One day Saul and a group of men set out to arrest Christians in **Damascus**, a city in ancient **Syria**.

On the road to Damascus something very strange happened to Saul. A light from heaven flashed around him. The light was so bright that he fell off his horse. He became blind.

Saul heard a voice, saying, "Saul, Saul, why are you against me?"

"Who are you?" Saul asked.

"I am Jesus," the voice said. "Go into the city and you will be told what to do."

The men traveling with Saul took him to Damascus. There, a Christian named **Ananias** came to visit Saul. Ananias said, "Brother Saul, the Lord Jesus sent me to you so that you might see again and be filled with the Holy Spirit." Ananias prayed for Saul.

At once Saul could see again.
He was baptized and became a Christian.
His life changed so much that he
taught the good news to people
in many lands. He became a leader
of the Christians and was known
as the Apostle **Paul**.

(Acts of the Apostles 9: 1 - 19)

God wants to change anything in us that
keeps us from loving Him and loving others.
That means God has given us the Holy Spirit to
help us change our wrong ways of thinking and acting.

How do you treat people you don't like?
Do you make fun of them? Do you ignore them?
Do you try to get them into trouble? Jesus teaches we
should love not only our friends but love our enemies
and pray for those who are against us.

We can ask the Holy Spirit to help us change how we think about others. We can ask the Holy Spirit to change the way we treat others.

Why did Katy change her mind about Mary? What did Paul do after he became a Christian? What would you like to change about yourself? Why?

New Words I Have Learned About

Pentecost	Apostle	Stephen	martyr
Damascus	Syria	Ananias	Paul

We Believe

The Holy Spirit Helps Us to Work Together
The Holy Spirit Helps Us to Share the Good News
The Holy Spirit Gives Us Courage
The Holy Spirit Helps Us to Love Others

Check Up

Answer the questions.

1. What is an Apostle? _____

_____

_____

_____

2. What did Peter and John do after the day of Pentecost?

_____

_____

_____

_____

3. Why is St. Stephen a martyr? _____

_____

_____

_____

4. What happened to Paul? _____

_____

_____

_____

UNIT 4 Families Share

Lesson 1 WE BELIEVE
Families Share Love

"Mom, when will Uncle John be here?" asked Mike. "He'll be here in time for dinner," his mother answered.

Mike liked listening to Uncle John's wonderful stories. Uncle John had grown up in Greece and knew about Mike's great-grandparents. He would tell many stories about them. Some stories were funny, others were sad. Sometimes Mike asked Uncle John to tell the same story over again.

Mike is finding out about people in his family who lived a long time ago. He enjoys learning who they were, what they were like, and how they lived. They are all part of his family tree.

Draw pictures of your grandparents, your parents, and yourself.

Grandparents   Grandparents

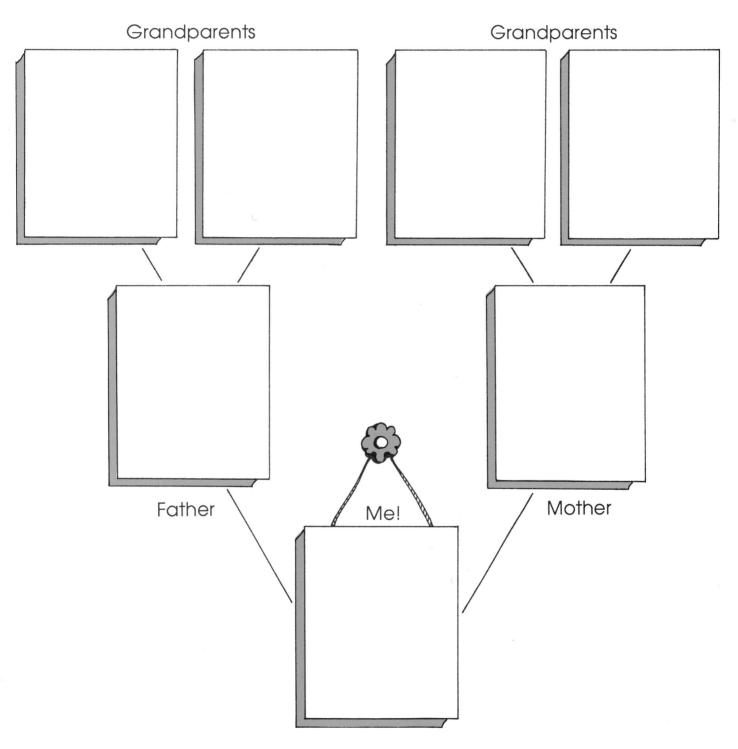

Father   Me!   Mother

Who else belongs to your family tree?

A Bible Story

The Family of Isaac

Isaac was the son of Abraham and Sarah. When Isaac was forty years old he married Rebecca. After a few years Isaac and Rebecca had two sons. They named the first-born Esau. They named the second son Jacob.

Jacob grew up to be a quiet man. He lived close to his parents and helped them in their old age. Esau became a hunter and lived outdoors. He was often gone for a long time.

One day Esau came home very hungry.
He found Jacob cooking bean soup.
"I'm starving. Give me some of that soup,"
asked Esau. Jacob answered, "I will, if you give
me your rights as the first-born son." In those
days the first-born son had the rights to all the
property of the family.

Esau agreed. He promised to give his rights
to Jacob, but later he changed his mind.
He became very angry and wanted to harm his
brother. Jacob had to escape to another country.
He lived there for a long time. He always hoped
that Esau would forget his anger.

After twenty years Jacob returned home with
many gifts. Esau came out to meet him.
The two brothers hugged each other and
became friends again.

(Genesis 25: 19 - 34)

We need our family. When someone hurts us, our parents help us to feel better. We are happy to tell our parents when we have done well on a test. When our parents are feeling bad, we can give them a hug.

In a family, everyone should care about one another. Families share love by talking together, playing together, and working together. Yet sometimes, people in a family hurt each other's feelings. When this happens, they should try to forgive one another.

Our family is the place where we learn how to love one another. Our family is the place where we learn about God and the world.

Lesson 2 WE BELIEVE
Family Meals Are Special

"I'll get it!" yelled Tina. She opened the door. "Hi, Aunt Stacy! Come on in. Do you know that everybody's coming today?" Her aunt replied, "And can you believe that Grandma and Grandpa have been married fifty years?"

Later that afternoon, everybody gathered around the dining room table. They said the Lord's Prayer together.

After the prayer, Tina's father stood up and said, "Mom, Dad, congratulations for fifty wonderful years." Everyone cheered, "Happy Anniversary!"

During dinner, Grandma and Grandpa told everyone how they met and fell in love. The dinner went on for a long time. Everyone was laughing and talking. No one wanted to leave the table.

The First Christians Shared Meals

The first Christians were like a family.
They shared many things. They prayed
together. They met in each other's homes to
share meals. Some brought bread or cheese.
Others brought fish or vegetables. Still others
brought oranges, figs, or honey.

    The Apostles also came to the meals.
They taught the Christians about Jesus.
They told the story about the Last Supper.
They talked about Christ's crucifixion and
His resurrection.

    During the meal, the Apostles blessed a loaf
of bread and a cup of wine as Christ did at the
Last Supper. The blessed bread and wine were
Holy Communion and was shared by everyone.
The Christians thanked God for all His
blessings. Joy and love filled their hearts.

God gives us food. We need food to live.
Some meals are fancy, like Tina's grandparents'
anniversary. Most are simple.

Whether a meal is fancy or simple,
mealtime should be more than a time to eat.
It is a time to pray. It is a time to share with
one another what happened during the day.
A family meal can remind us of the joy and love
shared by the first Christians.

Lesson 3 WE BELIEVE
Families Share Prayers

Mom passed out pencils and small pieces of paper and said, "Let's do something new for our family evening tonight. Think about each person in our family. Is there something you would like to thank them for? Write them a thank-you note."

Tom wrote, "Thank you Mom for making my lunch every day." Mary thanked her Dad for feeding her pet rabbit when she was not home. Dad's note to Mom said, "Thanks for being such a wonderful wife." Mom thanked the kids for helping to clean the house on Saturdays.

After everyone shared their thank-you notes, Dad read a story from the Bible. Then each one took a turn reading an evening prayer from a family prayer book.

A Bible Story

The Family of Cornelius

Cornelius lived in the days of the Apostles. He was a captain in the Roman army in **Caesarea**, a city in Palestine. He was a good man who loved God. Cornelius and his family prayed together and helped others.

One afternoon when Cornelius was praying, an angel came to him and said, "Cornelius, God is pleased with your prayers and your good works. Invite the Apostle Peter to your home and he will tell you about the good news." Cornelius obeyed the angel.

The Apostle Peter came to the home of Cornelius. There Peter spoke about Christ. Cornelius and his family listened carefully. While Peter was speaking the Holy Spirit filled the hearts of Cornelius, his wife, and children. They believed that Jesus is the Savior. They all prayed with Peter and were soon baptized.

(Acts of the Apostles chapter 10)

There are many times when a family can pray together. A family can say the Lord's Prayer before a meal. Prayers can be said when someone is sick or before going on a trip. Parents and children should also pray together when they are preparing to receive Holy Communion.

Whether we pray alone or as a family, we can use our own words to thank God or to ask for His help. If we do not know what to say, we can use a **prayer book**. A prayer book has many prayers for meals, bedtime, and special events.

Parents and children who pray together feel closer to God and to one another. We become more loving and forgiving toward each other when we pray together. Sharing prayers brings peace and joy in a family.

 (Activity) **Write a prayer for you and your family.**

Lesson 4 WE BELIEVE
Families Share Memories

"Look!" said George laughing. "This is when I got all wet at Niagara Falls. Do you remember the boat ride below the Falls?"

"Yes, I do," said his mother. "You should have kept the raincoat buttoned and your hood on!"

George's family was enjoying going through a photo album. It was fun looking at old pictures. One summer they had gone from Boston to Milwaukee for a friend's wedding. On the way back they traveled through Canada and visited Niagara Falls.

"What do you remember most about the trip, Claire?" asked Dad. "The big trampoline at the campground in Canada," answered Claire. "I wish we could have stayed there longer."

Mom said, "I liked the wedding best and the wonderful reception. What about you, Dad?"

"My favorite part was just being with all of you," Dad answered. "That vacation was something to remember."

The Story of a Saint

The Christians Remember St. Polycarp

St. Polycarp lived about a hundred years after Christ. He was the bishop of Christians in **Smyrna**, a city in **Asia Minor**. It was a time when the Roman governor was trying to destroy the Christian Church. He sent soldiers to arrest Christians and put them to death.

Bishop Polycarp was arrested too. The soldiers brought him to the governor at the stadium. "Give up your faith in Christ and I will release you," said the governor. "No," Polycarp replied. "How can I give up my Savior whom I have served for eighty-six years?"

The governor ordered the soldiers to take Polycarp away and to kill him.

The Christians took Polycarp's body and buried it with special care. They prayed to God and remembered what a good bishop Polycarp had been. After a year they met again on the day Polycarp died to remember his good example. Soon it became a custom for Christians to remember all the saints on the day they died and went to heaven.

Do you remember going on a vacation with your family? That's a family **memory**. Moving into a new home becomes a memory. Some memories are celebrated on certain days every year. On your birthday your family remembers the day you were born.

Families also have sad memories. It might be about someone who died. A family can remember that person in church with a **Memorial Service**. At a Memorial Service, a family brings a tray of boiled wheat sprinkled with powdered sugar. We pray that people who have died are in heaven. We ask God to forgive their sins and give them peace. Everyone sings that their memory may live on forever.

Activity Draw a picture of a family memory.

UNIT 4 Review

New Words I Have Learned About

Isaac	Rebecca	Esau
Jacob	Cornelius	Caesarea
prayer book	Polycarp	Smyrna
Asia Minor	memory	Memorial Service

We Believe

Families Share Love
Family Meals Are Special
Families Share Prayers
Families Share Memories

Check Up

Fill in the blanks.

1. Families share love by _____ , _____ ,
   and _____ together.

2. Everyone in a _____ should care about one another.

3. The first _____ were like a family.

4. Mealtime is also a time to _____ and to _____ .

5. Sharing prayers brings _____
   and _____ in a family.

6. Families have happy and sad _____ .

7. A _____ Service helps us to remember
   and pray for someone who has died.

UNIT 5 We Share in Church

Lesson 1 WE BELIEVE
We Share the Good News in the Liturgy

"We received a package today from our pen pals in Australia," Mr. Gibbons announced. Everyone in the class was curious. "Let's open it," said one of the students. Inside were a letter, some pictures, and a flag. "We'll have to display all these for everyone to see," the teacher said. "John, would you please read the letter?" John stood up and read,

"Dear friends in America,
    Thank you for your last letter. We enjoyed learning about San Francisco. Let us tell you about Australia. Our country is such a large island that it's one of the seven continents. You might think it's funny but here, winter begins in June and summer begins in December! People from all over the world have settled in our country. We hope you like the pictures of Australia, especially the koalas! In your next letter please tell us more about the United States.
            Your friends in Australia."

When John finished reading the letter, Mr. Gibbons asked the class, "How does it feel to receive news from children who live in another country? What news can we share with our pen pals?"

Sharing the Gospel

We share different kinds of news in different ways. Mr. Gibbons' class received interesting news about Australia. In the Divine Liturgy we share special news about God.

When the Liturgy begins, the priest lifts up the **Gospel Book** and says, "Blessed is the kingdom of the Father and the Son and the Holy Spirit." The priest then offers many prayers asking God for what we need in our lives. "Lord, have mercy" is sung after each prayer.

A little later the altar boys come out of the altar holding candles. The priest follows carrying the Gospel Book. He sings a hymn, "Come let us worship and bow before Christ." Then the priest and the altar boys return to the altar.

After the hymn "Holy God" is sung, the
chanter reads the **Epistle**. Then the priest
turns to the people and says, "Wisdom. Arise.
Let us hear the Holy Gospel." Everyone stands
and listens carefully. The priest holds the
Gospel Book and he reads the good news to us.
After the reading, "Glory to You, O Lord,
glory to You" is sung.

The Liturgy is a celebration of God's love which we receive through Christ. The Divine Liturgy has two parts. In the first part we listen to the Epistle and the Gospel readings. Gospel means good news. The Gospel Book tells us about the life of Jesus, the miracles He did, and what He taught. Epistle means letter. The Apostles wrote letters to teach us how to live God's way. The Epistle and the Gospel tell us that God loves us, that Jesus is the Son of God, and that Jesus came to save us. When we listen carefully to the good news, we learn how to live as Orthodox Christians.

Lesson 2 WE BELIEVE
We Share Holy Communion in the Liturgy

Anna and Grandma are baking bread today.

Anna: Why is bread so important, Grandma?

Grandma: Bread is a gift from God. It keeps us healthy and strong. Bread gives life to people everywhere.

Anna: What is prosforo? How different is it from the bread we usually bake?

Grandma: Prosforo is a special holy bread. It is very much like the bread we usually bake except that...

Anna: Except that we bring it to church.

Grandma: Yes, prosforo is our gift to God. The priest blesses it and it becomes the body of Christ.

Anna: And then we receive it as Holy Communion.

Grandma: Well, so you do know about prosforo after all! Shall we make some?

Sharing the Gifts of Bread and Wine

The second part of the Liturgy begins after the reading of the Gospel. The altar boys come out of the altar holding candles, a cross, and a censer. The priest follows bringing the gifts of bread and wine. He sings, "May the Lord God remember all of us in His kingdom always." The priest returns to the altar and places the gifts of bread and wine on the altar table.

At a special moment in the Liturgy, the priest offers the gifts of bread and wine to God and says, "We offer to You these gifts from Your own gifts." Everyone kneels to show respect. The priest asks God to send the Holy Spirit to bless the bread and wine. The power of the Holy Spirit changes the bread and wine into the body and blood of Christ. This is Holy Communion.

We sing, "We praise You. We bless You. We give thanks to You and we pray to You, Lord our God."

Before receiving Holy Communion, everyone prays the Lord's Prayer. Then the priest, holding the chalice, faces the congregation and says, "Approach with the fear of God, faith and love." We go to the priest slowly and quietly and we receive Holy Communion. After we share Holy Communion, we sing the hymn, "We have seen the true light." Soon the Liturgy ends.

God gave us the gifts of bread and wine.
People have made and eaten bread for a very
long time. Bread has been such an important
food that it is a symbol of life. Bread and wine
have often been a part of meals.

During the Liturgy we offer the gifts of bread
and wine to God to bless them. We receive
them as Holy Communion. We share these
gifts with one another. Holy Communion joins
us with Jesus. This sacrament reminds us that
we are one church family. When we receive
Holy Communion our hearts are filled with love
for Jesus and for one another.

Lesson **3** WE BELIEVE
We Share Holy Oil

Greg's sunburn hurt. "Why did I stay out in the sun so long?" he moaned. "Dad, can you make it stop?"

Greg's father gently applied a special lotion to his burned shoulders. The lotion made him feel comfortable. His father said, "Now you know what happens when you stay out in the sun too long. Keep your shoulders covered. In a few days you'll feel better."

The Sacrament of Holy Oil

In the Bible we read, "Is anyone sick?
He should call the priests who will pray and
anoint him with oil in the name of the Lord.
This prayer will heal the sick person.
The Lord will make him healthy and his sins will
be forgiven."

We all need courage and strength,
especially when we are sick.
Being close to God helps us to
become well.
The Sacrament of **Holy Oil**
brings us close to God.
This sacrament is a
special service for healing
and forgiveness through
God's power. It is
also called
Holy Unction.

The Sacrament of Holy Oil usually takes place on Holy Wednesday before Easter. It can also be done at any other time in church or at home. A small bowl of oil is placed on a table. The priest and the **chanter** sing hymns. The chanter helps the priest by singing or reading prayers and hymns. The priest prays for health, peace, and forgiveness for all the people. He asks God to bless the oil. The chanter reads seven Epistles. The priest reads seven Gospels.

At the end of the service, the priest **anoints** the face and hands of everyone with the Holy Oil. To anoint means to put Holy Oil on someone.

The Good Samaritan rubbed oil on the man who was hurt. In the same way, the lotion helped Greg's sunburn. During the Sacrament of Holy Oil we receive God's power to be healed and to be forgiven.

We get sick and we need to be healed. We also sin and we need to be forgiven. The Sacrament of Holy Oil is for all of us. When we receive Holy Oil, God fills us with the Holy Spirit. The Holy Spirit gives us strength and courage to live a healthy and good life.

Lesson 4 WE BELIEVE
We Share Holy Water

Mike was working on a school report about water. He was thinking about how water is used at home. He wrote, "I need water to take a shower and to brush my teeth. I drink water when I am thirsty. We use water to do the laundry and to water the garden."

Then he thought about water in nature. "Water keeps rivers flowing and helps to grow crops. Fish live in water. We skate on ponds when the water is frozen. I swim in the ocean during the summer. People sail their boats on the lake."

Mike became interested in his report. Now he had so many things to say about water. Water is all around us. Everything needs water to live. Water is a wonderful gift from God.

The Blessing of Water

The Orthodox Church has a service called the **Blessing of the Water**. This service can take place at church, at home, or anywhere. A bowl of water is placed on a table. The priest prays and asks God to bless the water. He dips a cross into the water and sings a hymn. God blesses the water and makes it the gift of Holy Water.

One of the prayers of the service says: "Hear us, O Lord, who was baptized in the Jordan River and blessed the water. Bless all of us who

bow our heads to show that we are Your
servants. Fill us with Your holiness when we
drink this water and when we are sprinkled with
it. O Lord, let this water make our souls and
bodies healthy. Amen."

At the end of the service we kiss the cross
and the priest sprinkles Holy Water on us.
The priest also sprinkles Holy Water around the
church or the house. Sometimes Holy Water is
kept at home in a small bottle to drink or
sprinkle on special occasions.

God gave us water when He made the world.
All plants and animals need water to live.
Water also cleans things that are dirty.

During the Blessing of Water we remember
that God gave us water to live and to keep
ourselves clean. Being sprinkled with Holy
Water, or drinking it, is a symbol of being
blessed by God. It reminds us that we must try
to keep ourselves clean and to stay away from
sins. God's blessing helps us to have good
thoughts and to live God's way.

124

Activity Circle the words hidden in the puzzle.

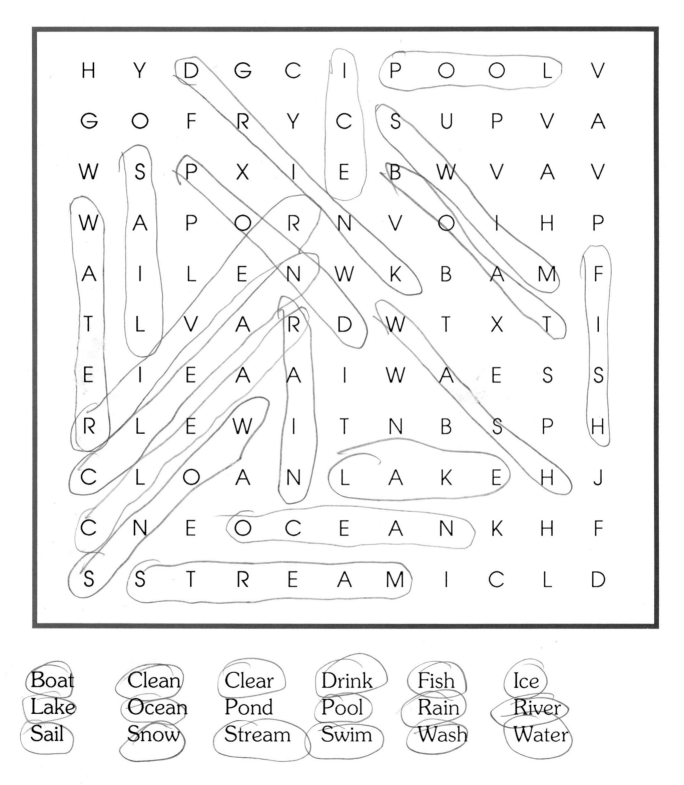

H	Y	D	G	C	I	P	O	O	L	V
G	O	F	R	Y	C	S	U	P	V	A
W	S	P	X	I	E	B	W	V	A	V
W	A	P	O	R	N	V	O	I	H	P
A	I	L	E	N	W	K	B	A	M	F
T	L	V	A	R	D	W	T	X	T	I
E	I	E	A	A	I	W	A	E	S	S
R	L	E	W	I	T	N	B	S	P	H
C	L	O	A	N	L	A	K	E	H	J
C	N	E	O	C	E	A	N	K	H	F
S	S	T	R	E	A	M	I	C	L	D

Boat   Clean   Clear   Drink   Fish   Ice
Lake   Ocean   Pond   Pool   Rain   River
Sail   Snow   Stream   Swim   Wash   Water

UNIT 5 Review

New Words I Have Learned About

Gospel Book	Epistle	Holy Oil
Holy Unction	chanter	anoint
	Blessing of the Water	

We Believe

We Share the Good News in the Liturgy
We Share Holy Communion in the Liturgy
We Share Holy Oil
We Share Holy Water

Check Up

Complete the crossword puzzle.

Across
1. Sacrament for healing.
4. It means letter.
6. It means good news.
7. In a hymn we sing, "We _____ You."

Down
2. A celebration of God's love.
3. It is sprinkled around the house.
5. A special bread used in Holy Communion.

UNIT 6 Sharing in the World

Lesson 1 WE BELIEVE
We Share Our Faith

Alex is preparing a Church school report on the
Orthodox Church in Africa. He is talking with Joseph,
a student at Holy Cross seminary.

   Alex: Where are you from, Joseph?

Joseph: I am from Uganda, a country in Africa.

   Alex: Have you always been an Orthodox Christian?

Joseph: Yes. My whole family is Orthodox.
My grandfather is a priest.

   Alex: Your grandfather! How did he become Orthodox?

Joseph: He met a group of Orthodox Christians who had traveled
to Africa. They told him about Christ and the
Orthodox Church. He believed in Jesus and joined
the Orthodox Church.

Alex: What do the churches look like in Africa?

Joseph: In big cities they look like churches in America. In small villages they are very different. Sometimes they are just grass huts.

Alex: Do they have icons?

Joseph: Sure, we have icons. We celebrate the same Divine Liturgy. We have the same sacraments. We believe the same things about Jesus that you do.

Alex: Thank you Joseph. I've learned a lot today.

The Travels of the Apostle Paul

The Apostle Paul was chosen by Christ to bring the good news to people living in faraway lands. He spent many years talking to people about Christ in **Syria** and Palestine.

Paul also went to the island of **Cyprus**. From Cyprus he traveled to the southern coast of Asia Minor. Everywhere he went, the Apostle Paul told people about Jesus. He taught them how to live according to the good news.

Later Paul went on a longer trip. He traveled through Asia Minor to a city called **Troas**. From Troas he crossed the **Aegean Sea** and came to **Philippi**, a city in northern Greece.

From there the Apostle visited many cities throughout Greece. He went to Thessalonike, **Athens**, and **Corinth**. On his way back to Jerusalem, Paul said, "I only want to complete my mission and finish the work that Jesus gave me to do. This mission is to tell all people the good news about God."

Wherever Paul went, people listened to him. Many became Christians. They joined together and started churches. Before he left, Paul chose leaders for the new churches. Later, he wrote letters to those new Christians to guide them in their Christian lives. As you have learned, these letters are called epistles.

The people who told Joseph's grandfather about Christ and the Orthodox Church were **missionaries**. The Apostle Paul was a missionary, too. Missionaries are people who travel from place to place to teach the good news about Jesus. Their work is called a **mission**.

You too, have a mission. You can share the good news about Christ and the Church with others. You do not have to travel to another country. You can share your **faith** in Jesus anywhere. Our faith is believing that Jesus is our Savior and that He brings us close to God. If you have a friend who does not go to church, you can invite your friend to your church. When someone asks you a question about the Orthodox Church, try to answer it! In these ways you share your faith.

Lesson 2 WE BELIEVE
We Share Our Love

Write your own words to tell this story.

_____

_____

_____

_____

_____

_____

_____

_____

_____

_____

_____

_____

_____

_____

_____

The Story of a Saint

The Unmercenary Brothers

Many years after Christ, two brothers were born to a rich family in Asia Minor. They were named Cosmas and Damian. They went to school together to study medicine. In their last year of school, they heard about Jesus and were baptized.

After they became doctors, Cosmas and Damian made an important decision. They decided to take care of sick people without charging them any money. They also spoke to them about Christ. They healed the sick with medicine and prayer.

Cosmas and Damian helped many people during their long lives. After they died, they were remembered for their kindness. The people called them **Holy Unmercenaries**. The word **mercenary** means to serve others only for money. The word "unmercenary" means just the opposite, someone who serves others only out of kindness and love. The Church honors Cosmas and Damian as saints.

You know that sharing means giving part of what you have to another person. God shared His love with all people by sending His Son Jesus to the world. Because God shared His love with us, we should share our love with others.

Jesus said, "I give you a new commandment, love one another. As I have loved you, so you must love one another. If you love one another, then everyone will know that you are my disciples."

When you share your love, something very special happens. The more you love, the more love you have inside your heart. Think of a time when you gave or said something to another person to show your love. How did you feel?

Lesson 3 WE BELIEVE
We Share What We Have

On a cold night in Philadelphia, the family car stopped at a traffic light. Trevor said quickly, "Dad, look! There's a man sleeping on the sidewalk." "I see him," said Mr. Ferrell, "he's one of the homeless people."

"But Dad, it's so cold out. Let's go home and get him a blanket." When they returned, Trevor walked up to the homeless man and asked, "Want a blanket, mister?"

The man took the blanket and said, "God bless you."

Soon Trevor, his family, and their friends were giving away blankets, clothes, and even food. Their story was on television and in newspapers all around the country. Many people sent Trevor food, clothing, and money to be given away. In a short time, people in other cities began helping the homeless people in the same way.

The Story of a Saint

St. Nicholas Helps a Poor Family

About three hundred years after Christ, there was a man named Nicholas. He was the Bishop of **Myra**, a city in Asia Minor. The people loved him and he loved all the people. His smile gave hope to those who were sad. His gifts brought joy to children.

Also in Myra, lived a very poor family. The father was sad and very worried. He could not buy food for his family. And how could he hope to have his three daughters married? He was ready to do anything for money.

When Bishop Nicholas heard about this family he thought of a plan to help them. One evening, when no one was looking, he tossed a bag of gold coins through an open window of their house. The family was very surprised and they danced with joy. On the second evening Bishop Nicholas tossed another bag of gold coins into the house. On the third evening the family was hiding outside and caught the secret giver with yet another bag of gold coins. They thanked Bishop Nicholas from their hearts. Now they could buy food and clothes. There was also enough money to give to each daughter on her wedding day.

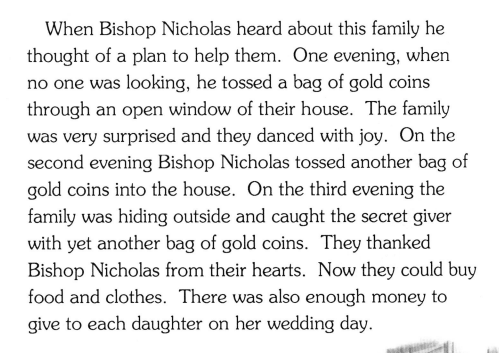

Activity What can Christians do to show love to the people in these pictures? Write your answer.

_____

_____

_____

_____

_____

_____

_____

_____

_____

_____

_____

_____

_____

_____

_____

_____

_____

Lesson 4 WE BELIEVE
We Work for Justice

Joanna, Cindy, and their friends were playing jump rope. Joanna and Cindy were swinging the rope. Sometimes three girls would jump in at once. Everyone was laughing and having fun.

Everyone, except Teresa. Twice she tried to jump in and twice she was pushed away. "You don't know how!" said Joanna.

"She doesn't speak English, she can't play," added Cindy. But Teresa understood every word they said. She felt hurt and lonely.

Stephanie decided to speak up, "It's not fair! Why don't you let her play like everyone else? You're so mean!" Stephanie took the rope from Joanna, and she said to Teresa, "Go on Teresa! Take a turn." Teresa jumped in. The others followed. Soon everyone was laughing and jumping rope again. Now Teresa had as much fun as anyone else.

In the Sermon on the Mount, Christ taught
His disciples to practice **justice**. Justice means
being fair to others and doing what is right
according to God. Christ told His disciples that
above everything else they should think about
God and what God wants them to do.

Jesus said,
"Happy are those
whose greatest desire
is to do what God asks!"
A just person treats others
with fairness and respect.
A just person is good and
lives as God wants him to.
He is also called **righteous**
because he does what
is right.

In the Bible we learn that Cornelius, the Roman
captain, was such a person. He was a good and just
man because he loved God and treated
everyone with kindness.
The Bible teaches us to practice what is good, fair,
and right. We read in the Bible, "Fill your
minds with those things that are good, true, and right.
Do what you have learned. And God
who gives peace will be with you."

Christians are taught to practice justice and to do what is right every day. Children should behave well, even when their parents are not looking.

Why was Stephanie upset with Joanna and Cindy? Have you ever felt like Teresa? No one should be left out because of his color, religion, language, or ability. All people deserve to be treated fairly. When we are fair with one another everybody is happy.

Christians must also work for justice in all parts of the world. When everyone works for justice there is more freedom and peace in the world.

 **Activity** Unscramble the words below and write the letters in the squares. Then unscramble the circled letters to answer the clue.

EEDRFOM

ECAPE

EJITUSC

EHRITGOSU

ESSAIFRN

ETCRPES

People who believe in Jesus Christ.

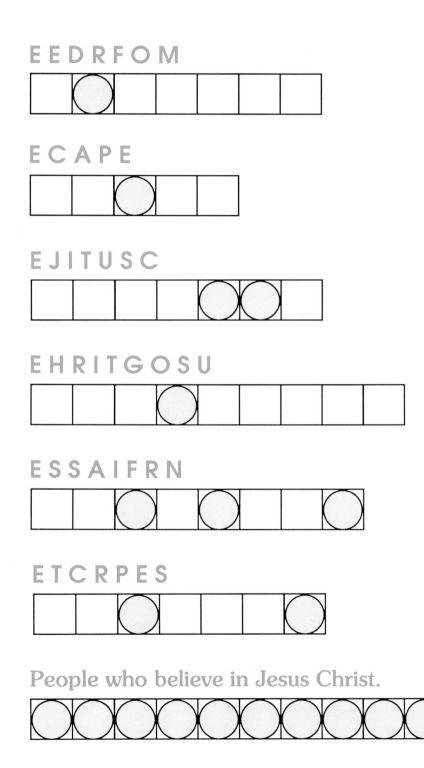

UNIT 6 Review

New Words I Have Learned About

Syria	Cyprus	Troas	Aegean Sea
Philippi	Athens	Corinth	righteous
missionary	faith	justice	Holy Unmercenaries
mercenary	Myra	mission	

We Believe

We Share Our Faith
We Share Our Love
We Share What We Have
We Work for Justice

Please Help the Poor

148

Check Up

Fill in the blanks.

1. St. Paul helped the Christians form _____ .

2. _____ share the good news

   about _____ in other countries.

3. Our _____ is believing that Jesus is the Savior.

4. Cosmas and Damian served others only out of _____

   and _____ .

5. The poor family in Myra was helped by _____ .

6. Treating all people fairly is practicing _____ .

7. The Bible teaches us to practice what is _____ ,

   _____ , and _____ .

8. When we are _____ with one another everyone

   is happy.

Feast Days
to Share God's Gifts

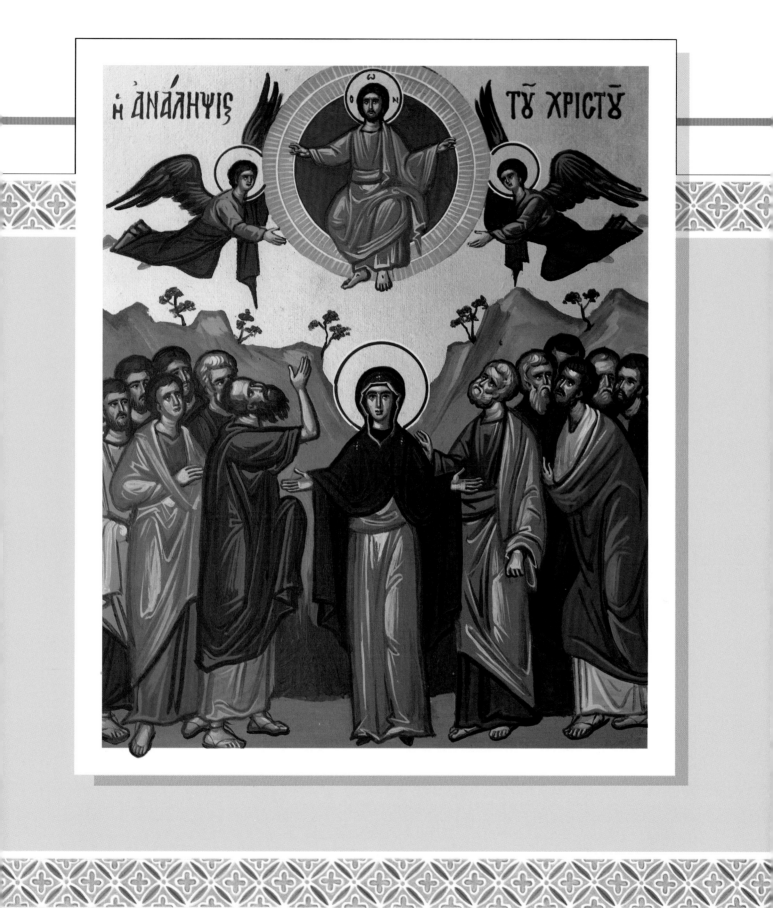

WE BELIEVE
Our Savior Is Born

Christmas is a holy day of joy. The angel announced to the shepherds, "I am here with good news for you, which will bring great joy to all the people. This very day in Bethlehem your Savior was born, Christ the Lord." Angels sang when Christ was born. The shepherds and wise men were the first to share the good news. God sent us His son, our Savior.

At Christmas, we celebrate God's love. God loved the world so much that He shared His only son with us. We **rejoice** because God sent His son Jesus to save us. To rejoice means to feel great joy.

Just as God shared His love with us, we share our love and joy with others. How can we thank God for sharing His love? What can we do to share our love and joy with others?

(Activity) **Read the hymn for Christmas and answer the questions.**

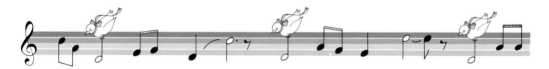

O Christ our God, Your birth has shone the light of knowledge upon the world. At Your birth, those who worshipped the stars, were taught by a star to worship You, the Sun of Righteousness, and to know You as a dawn from heaven. Lord, glory to You.

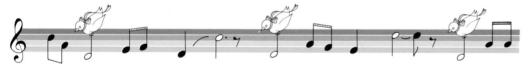

What shines upon the world at Christmas? _____

_____

_____

How did the wise men learn about the birth of Jesus?

_____

What did they learn? _____

_____

WE BELIEVE
Icons Help Us to Worship

Icons are important to Orthodox Christians. They are pictures of Christ and the saints. Icons tell us about their lives. Icons remind us that Christ and the saints were real people. Orthodox Christians **venerate** icons by kissing them and burning incense and candles near them. To venerate icons is to show respect for Jesus and the saints.

We do not worship icons. We worship God and Christ. Icons help us to worship. They remind us of what God has done for us through Jesus and the saints.

On the first Sunday of **Great Lent**, the Sunday of Orthodoxy, we celebrate the use of icons in the Orthodox Church. Great Lent is the period of time that lasts forty days before Holy Week and Easter.

On the Sunday of Orthodoxy the priest, the altar boys, even children and adults, carry icons around the church.

(Activity) **Read the hymn for the Sunday of Orthodoxy and answer the questions.**

We venerate Your holy icon, loving Lord, asking You, Christ our God, to forgive our sins.
By Your will You chose to be crucified as a man, to rescue those whom You created from the slavery of the enemy.
Therefore, with thanks we sing to You,
"You have filled all things with joy, our Savior, coming to save the world."

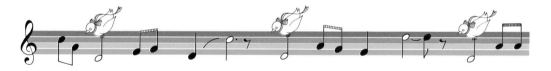

Whose icon do we venerate? _____

_____

Why did Christ die on the Cross? _____

_____

What do we sing to Christ? _____

_____

The Victory of the Icons

More than a thousand years ago, the Emperor of **Constantinople** made a law against owning icons. He decided it was wrong to venerate pictures of Christ and the saints. He ordered soldiers to remove them from churches and homes.

Many people disagreed with the new law and tried to stop the soldiers. Some people were killed. More were put in jail. Others hid their icons.

Some fifty years later **Empress Irene** was on the throne. She loved icons. She made plans to have a special meeting, called a **council**. Many bishops came to the council. They decided that people could venerate icons because Jesus and the saints were real persons.

After the council, people still fought and argued about icons. Empress Irene died, and the emperors after her tried again to remove icons from the churches and homes. The emperors ordered soldiers to destroy icons and put people in jail. Again, people hid their icons.

Many years passed and a new empress, **Empress Theodora**, ordered the return of all the icons to the churches. On the first Sunday of Great Lent, the icons were carried through the streets and brought back to the main church of **St. Sophia**. Everyone celebrated the victory of the icons. It was a great day for the Orthodox faith. That is why this day is called the Sunday of Orthodoxy.

WE BELIEVE
Christ Rose from the Dead

Jesus is the Son of God. He died and He rose from the dead to destroy the power of death. Now people do not have to be afraid of death because when we die we live with Jesus. We believe by having faith in Jesus we live forever.

Look at the icon of the Resurrection of Christ. He is lifting Adam and Eve out of the tombs. The others are righteous people like Abraham and Moses who lived before Jesus and were waiting for the Savior. The locks and the broken doors remind us that Christ destroyed the power of death.

We sing the hymns of Easter for forty days because Easter is the most important feast of the Church. During this time we greet others, "Christ is Risen!" They answer, "Truly He is Risen!"

Read this Easter hymn and answer the questions.

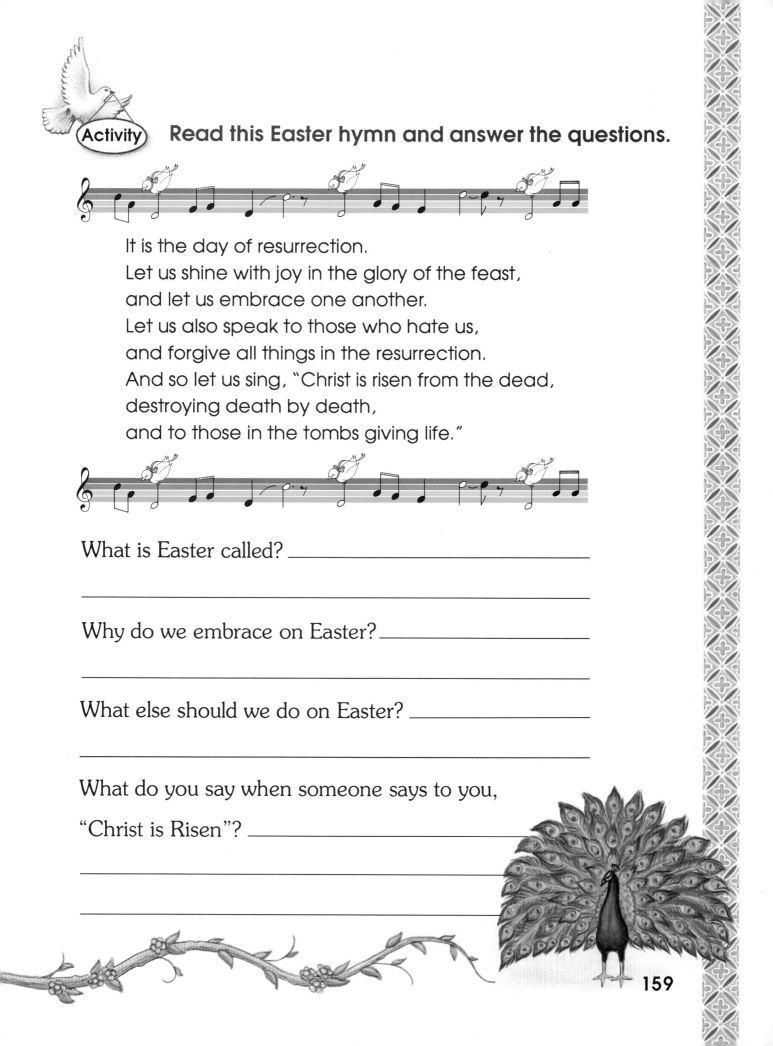

It is the day of resurrection.
Let us shine with joy in the glory of the feast,
and let us embrace one another.
Let us also speak to those who hate us,
and forgive all things in the resurrection.
And so let us sing, "Christ is risen from the dead,
destroying death by death,
and to those in the tombs giving life."

What is Easter called? _____

_____

Why do we embrace on Easter? _____

_____

What else should we do on Easter? _____

_____

What do you say when someone says to you,

"Christ is Risen"? _____

_____

_____

Ascension

WE BELIEVE
Christ Ascended to Heaven

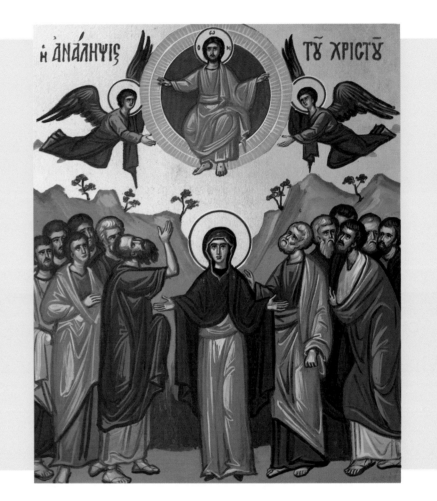

For forty days after His resurrection, Jesus talked with His disciples many times. Jesus told them, "Do not leave Jerusalem. You will receive the Holy Spirit who will fill you with strength."

On the fortieth day, the disciples met with Christ for the last time. Christ told them, "Go to all people and make them my disciples. Baptize them in the name of the Father, the Son, and the Holy Spirit. Teach them to obey everything that I have commanded you. I will be with you always."

Then Jesus raised His hands and blessed the disciples. As He was blessing them, they saw Jesus **ascend** to heaven until a cloud hid Him from their sight. To ascend means to go up. The Feast of the Ascension celebrates Christ going up to heaven. It is celebrated on a Thursday, forty days after Easter.

Activity **Read the hymn for Ascension and answer the questions.**

You ascended in glory, Christ our God, making Your disciples glad by promising to send the Holy Spirit to them.
When You blessed them, they knew that You are the Son of God, the Savior of the world.

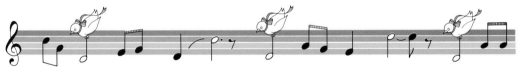

What does ascend mean?_____

_____

What did Christ promise to send to the disciples? _____

_____

Who is Christ? _____

_____

Pentecost

WE BELIEVE
We Share the Holy Spirit

Christ sent the Holy Spirit to His disciples on the day of Pentecost. The Holy Spirit filled them with the courage to tell the good news. On that day, Peter said to a crowd of people, "Be baptized in the name of Jesus Christ so that your sins will be forgiven, and you will receive God's gift, the Holy Spirit." On that day three thousand people were baptized and received the Holy Spirit.

The Feast of Pentecost falls on a Sunday, fifty days after Easter. There is a special service after the Divine Liturgy. During the service we kneel three times while the priest reads three long prayers. In the prayers we ask God to forgive our sins and to give us the Holy Spirit.

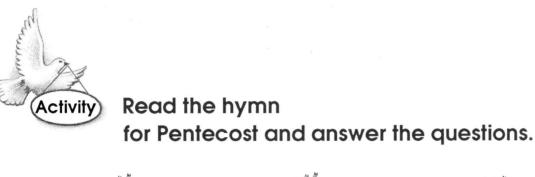

Activity Read the hymn for Pentecost and answer the questions.

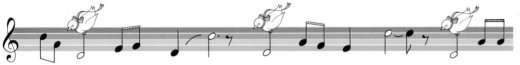

Blessed are You, O Christ our God, who filled the
fishermen with wisdom, by sending the Holy Spirit
to them.
Through the disciples You drew the whole world
into a net.
Loving Lord, glory to You.

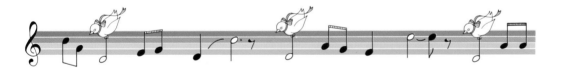

Who are the fishermen? _____

_____

What did Christ fill the disciples with? _____

_____

How did Christ do that? _____

_____

What did Christ do through the disciples? _____

_____

Hymns *and* Songs

The Wealthy Can Become Poor (Hymn for the "Blessing of the Five Loaves")

Those in whom wealth abounds can poor and
hungry be.
But those who eagerly seek the Lord,
never shall in want be
of any blessing.

Your Birth O Christ (Hymn of Christmas)

Your Birth O Christ our God did shine
upon the world.
And through the light of wisdom
illumined the universe.
And to those who held the stars in worship
did through a star learn to worship You.
Worship You, the sun of righteousness,
and came to know
You the Light from on high.
Glory to You O Lord.

Blessed Are You O Christ (Hymn of Pentecost)

O blessed are You, O Christ our God.
Who by sending down,
the Holy Spirit upon them,
made the fishermen wise and through them,
illumined the world.
And to You, the universe was ever drawn.
All glo–ry to You O Lord.

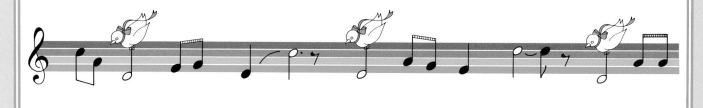

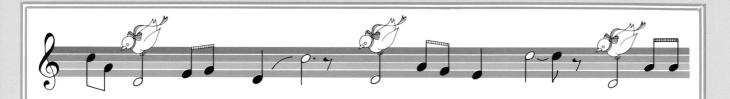

Praise The Lord (Communion Hymn)

Praise.
Praise the Lord.
From the heavens.
Praise Him, praise Him.
In the high-est, the highest.
Allelu–i–a.

Sharing's In The Giving (Theme Song)

Sharing is believing that getting's in the giving.
Sharing in a Christian way.
Sharing is believing that Jesus does the giving
in a saving way.

(chorus)
Open up your hearts, sharing's in the giving.
Open up your hearts, Jesus gives the meaning,
Living, sharing, giving!

Abraham was sitting down un–der a tree,
waiting for the sun to go down.
He looked out o'er the fields, three
angels went to greet him,
"Good tidings for you will be found."

(chorus)

Sharing is believing that getting's in the giving.
Sharing in a Christian way.
Sharing is believing that Jesus does the giving
in a saving way.

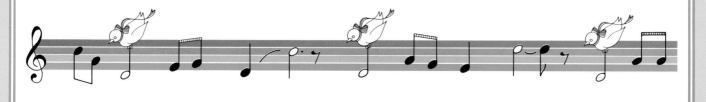

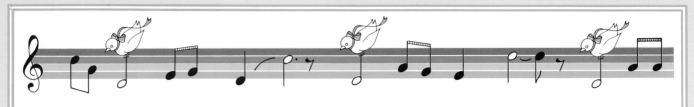

Hymns and Songs

There's Nothing That God Cannot Do

I will lift up my eyes unto the Lord.
He is my life and my song.
I will call upon Him and praise His Name
all of my life long.

(chorus)
For there's nothing that God cannot do!
His ways are much higher than mine and yours too!
He shows mercy to those who honor Him!
For there's nothing that God cannot do!

An angel spoke to Ma–ry, a long time ago.
She replied,
"I am the Lord's servant, now
let these things be so."

(chorus)

The incense goes up, and so do our prayers
For love, joy, and peace to each one.
For peace, patience, kindness, for all of these things,
Yes all of these things are pro– –mised!

(chorus)

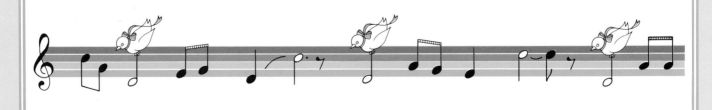

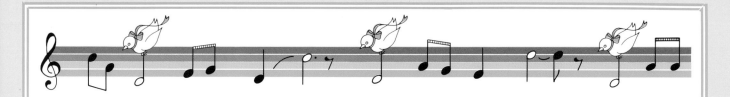

Give Thanks

Give thanks, give thanks, give thanks to the Lord!
Give thanks to the Lord for loving me.
Thank you Father for your Son.
I can share with ev'ryone.
Give thanks, give thanks, give thanks to the Lord!
Give thanks to the Lord for lov–ing me.

Give thanks, give thanks, give thanks to the Lord!
Give thanks to the Lord for blessing me, for lov–ing me.*
Thank you Father for your Son.
I can share with ev'ryone.
Give thanks, give thanks, give thanks to the Lord!
Give thanks to the Lord for bles–sing me.

Come sing your praises to the Lord!
Sing your praises loud and strong, for your Good
News, for my cross to bear, for blessing me,
for lov–ing me.
Thank you Father for your Son.
I can share with ev'ryone.
Give thanks, give thanks, give thanks to the Lord!
Give thanks to the Lord for lov–ing me.

*additional lyrics to be added for verses
(verse 3) for my cross to bear
(verse 4) for your Good News.

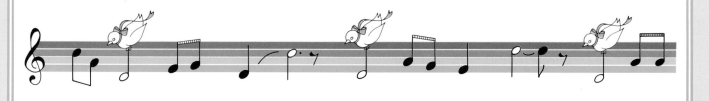

Glossary

Geographic locations can be found on the maps, pages 170 and 171.

Aegean Sea - Sea located between Greece and Asia Minor. p. 170

Ananias - Name of a Christian who visited Saul in Damascus. p. 77

anoint - To put Holy Oil on someone. p.119

Apostle - A person who is sent out to share the good news. p. 60

ascend - To go up. p. 161

Ascension - The day when Jesus went to heaven. It is celebrated forty days after Easter. p. 160

Asia Minor - Land by the Aegean Sea which Paul visited during his travels. p.132

Athens - City in Greece which Paul visited during his travels. p. 133

Blessing of the Five Loaves - A special church service that reminds us of the day when Jesus fed 5,000 people. p. 46

Blessing of the Water - A special church service when the priest asks God to bless the water and make it the gift of Holy Water. p. 122

Caesarea - A city in Palestine where Cornelius lived. p. 94

Canaan - The land that God promised to Abraham and his people. Abraham and Sarah lived there when the three angels visited them. p. 4

chanter - A person who helps the priest by singing hymns. p. 119

Christ - The greatest leader chosen by God to save the world. He is the Son of God and the Savior. p. 38

Corinth - A city in Greece which Paul visited during his travels. p. 133

Cornelius - A captain in the Roman army, who was baptized by the Apostle Peter. p. 94

council - A special meeting. p. 156

covenant - When two people make promises to each other. p. 16

Cyprus - An island off Asia Minor, which Paul visited during his travels. p. 132

Damascus - A city in ancient Syria where Saul went to arrest Christians. p. 76

Empress Irene - Called a council to decide whether people could venerate icons. p. 156

Empress Theodora - Ordered the return of all the icons to the churches. p. 157

epistle - Means letter. The Apostles wrote epistles to teach us how to live God's way. p. 111

Esau - The first-born son of Isaac and Rebecca. p. 86

faith - Our faith is believing that Jesus is our Savior and that He brings us closer to God. p. 134

Fishers of People - Name that Jesus gave to His first disciples. It means that they were His helpers. From then on they would teach people to live God's way. p. 40

God's Law - The Ten Commandments and other rules that God gave to Moses on Mount Sinai. p. 20

Golgotha - Name of the place near Jerusalem where Jesus and two other prisoners were crucified. p. 51

Gospel Book - A special part of the Bible that tells us about the life of Jesus. p. 110

governor - Leader of a small part of a country. p. 50

Great Lent - The forty-day period before Holy Week and Easter. p. 154

Holy Oil - A sacrament. A special church service for healing and forgiveness through

God's power. Also called the Sacrament of Holy Unction. p. 118

Holy Unction - See Holy Oil. p. 118

Holy Unmercenaries - Saint Cosmas and Saint Damian. They were Christian doctors who helped others only out of kindness and love, not for money. p. 137

hospitality - Sharing friendship and food with guests. p. 6

Jacob - The second son of Isaac and Rebecca. p. 86

justice - Being fair to others and doing what is right according to God's Law. p. 144

martyr - A saint who dies for his faith. p. 71

Memorial Service - A church service that helps the family and friends remember and pray for someone who died. p. 102

memory - Remembering someone or something. p. 102

mercenary - a person who does something only for money. p. 137

mission - The work done by missionaries. p. 134

missionaries - People who travel to teach the good news about Jesus. p. 134

Mount Sinai - Mountain where God gave the Ten Commandments and other rules to Moses. p. 20

Myra - A city in Asia Minor where Bishop Nicholas lived. p. 140

Paul - An Apostle who traveled to many places to teach the good news about Jesus. p. 77

Pentecost - The day when the disciples were filled with the Holy Spirit. It is celebrated fifty days after Easter. p. 59

Philippi - A city in northern Greece which Paul visited during his travels. p. 132

Pontius Pilate - The Roman governor who let the soldiers take Jesus to crucify Him. p. 50

prayer book - A book of prayers for meals, bedtime, and special events. p. 96

Rebecca - Wife of Isaac, mother of Esau and Jacob. p. 86

rejoice - To feel a great joy. p. 152

righteous - A person who does what is right. p. 145

Saint Polycarp - Bishop of Smyrna who died for his faith. p. 100

Saint Sophia - Name of the church in Constantinople where the people first celebrated the victory of the icons. p. 157

Saint Stephen - The first martyr of the Christian church. p. 70

Saul - Name of Paul before he became a Christian. p. 76

Sea of Galilee - A large lake in Galilee. p. 40

seminary - A school where men study to become priests. p. 13

Smyrna - A city in Asia Minor where Bishop Polycarp lived. p. 100

synagogue - A place where the Hebrew people went to pray. p. 36

Syria - A country that Paul visited during his travels. p. 132

tabernacle - A special tent where Moses and the people could pray when they were crossing the desert. p. 27

Troas - A city in Asia Minor that Paul visited during his travels. p. 132

venerate - To show respect. p. 154

Greece and Asia Minor

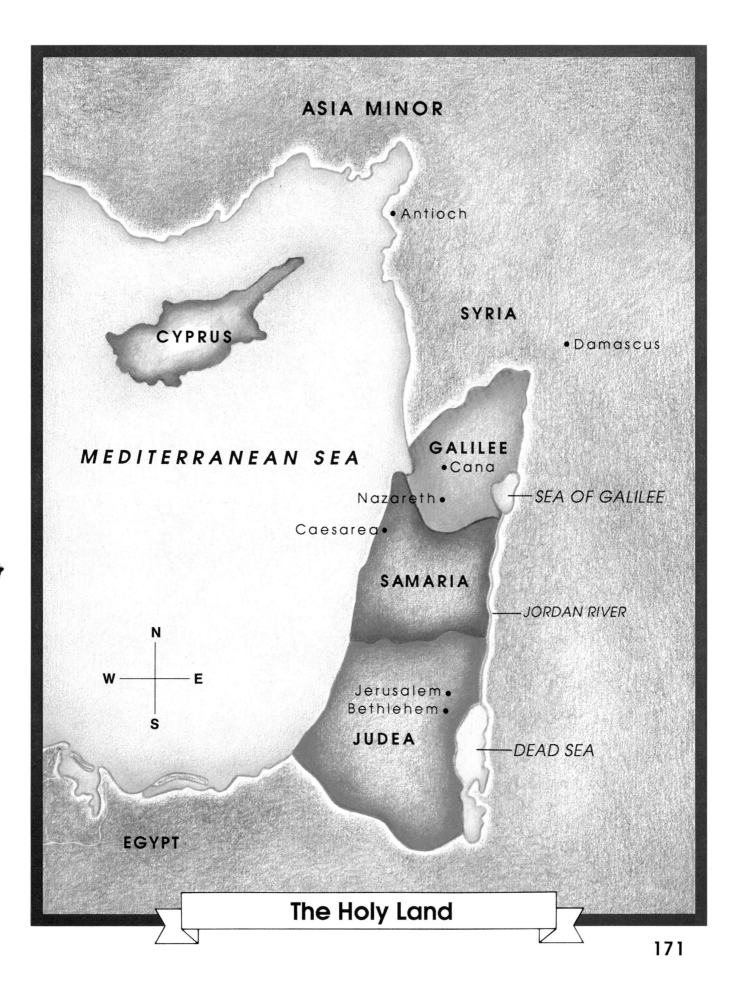

The Holy Land

CREDITS

Cover Photo: Alan Penn for the Greek Orthodox Church
Bible and Saint Story Art: Deb Troyer Bunnell
Lesson Art: Deb Troyer Bunnell, Lane Yerkes
Unit Review Art: Lane Yerkes
Maps: Jacqueline Haven

Design Studio of Jacqueline Haven
Photo Research: Christiane Angeli

II-III: Jim Whitmer for the Greek Orthodox Church; Iconographer C. Youssis; Michael Paras; Jim Whitmer; Jim Whitmer for the Greek Orthodox Church; Icon courtesy Mr. and Mrs. Ernest Villas; Icon courtesy Dormition Church, Somerville, MA.

Unit 1 IV: Jim Whitmer for the Greek Orthodox Church.
1: t. Icon courtesy Holy Cross Greek Orthodox School of Theology; b. Jim Whitmer for the Greek Orthodox Church.

Lesson 1 3: Elizabeth Crews/Stock, Boston.
6: Icon courtesy Holy Cross Greek Orthodox School of Theology. 7: Frank Siteman/Stock, Boston.
Lesson 2 12: Jim Whitmer for the Greek Orthodox Church.
Lesson 3 13: Areti Bratsis. 16: Bob Daemmrich/Stock, Boston.
Lesson 4 18: Michael Weisbrot/Stock, Boston.
21: Icon courtesy Tony Vrame. 22,23: Jim Whitmer for the Greek Orthodox Church.
Lesson 5 28: Jim Whitmer for the Greek Orthodox Church.

Unit 2 32: Addison Geary/Stock, Boston.
33: Iconographer C. Youssis; Jim Whitmer.

Lesson 1 38: Iconographer C. Youssis.
Lesson 2 39: Paul Fortin/Stock,Boston.
42: Kevin Horan/Stock, Boston.
Lesson 3 43: Peter Menzel/Stock, Boston.
46: Areti Bratsis.
Lesson 4 49: Courtesy Melnius Publishing Company, Tom DeWall photographer.
52: Addison Geary/Stock, Boston. 53: Jim Whitmer.

Unit 3 57: t. Icon courtesy St. Athanasios Church, Arlington, MA; b. Michael Paras.

Lesson 1 58: Frank Wing/Stock, Boston.
62: Michael Paras.
Lesson 2 64: Jim Whitmer for the Greek Orthodox Church. 68: Bill Gallery/Stock, Boston
Lesson 3 70: Icon courtesy St. Athanasios Church, Arlington, MA. 72: Frank Wing/Stock, Boston.
Lesson 4 74: Miro Vintoniv/Stock, Boston.
75: Frank Siteman/Stock, Boston. 78: Ellis Herwig/Stock, Boston. 79: Cary Wolinsky/Stock, Boston

Unit 4 82: t. Lawrence Migdale/Stock, Boston;
b. Jim Whitmer. 83: Jim Whitmer.

Lesson 1 84: Lawrence Migdale/Stock, Boston.
88: Jim Whitmer.
Lesson 2 89, 92: Jim Whitmer.
Lesson 3 93, 96: Jim Whitmer.
Lesson 4 98-99: Greg Cranna/Stock Boston.
99 (inset): Courtesy Fr. Theodore Stylianopoulos.

100: Courtesy Holy Transfiguration Monastery, Brookline, MA. 102: Tony Vrame.

Unit 5 106: Jim Whitmer for the Greek Orthodox Church.
107: t. Michael Paras; b. Jim Whitmer for the Greek Orthodox Church.

Lesson 1 109: John Cancalosi/Stock, Boston.
110, 111, 112: Jim Whitmer for the Greek Orthodox Church.
Lesson 2 114, 115: Jim Whitmer for the Greek Orthodox Church. 116: Laszlo Regos.
Lesson 3 118: Tom Styczynski for the Greek Orthodox Church. 119: Michael Paras.
120: Bob Daemmrich/Stock, Boston.
Lesson 4 121: Steve Weber/Stock, Boston.
122, 123, 124: Jim Whitmer for the Greek Orthodox Church.

Unit 6 128: Courtesy Merilynn Kouris.
129: t. Icon courtesy Mr. and Mrs. Ernest Villas;
b. Bob Daemmrich/Stock, Boston.

Lesson 1 130: Areti Bratsis. 131: Courtesy Merilynn Kouris. 134: Tom Styczynski for the Greek Orthodox Church.
Lesson 2 136: Icon courtesy Dormition Church, Somerville, MA. 138: Bob Daemmrich/Stock, Boston.
Lesson 3 139: Courtesy The Philadelphia Inquirer, Rob Clark Jr. photographer. 140: Icon courtesy Mr. and Mrs. Ernest Villas. 142: t. J.M. Delevingne/ Stock, Boston; m. Cary Wolinsky/Stock, Boston; b. Jim Whitmer/Stock, Boston.
Lesson 4 143: Jean Claude Lejeune/Stock, Boston. 146: Jerry Howard/Stock, Boston.

Feast Days to Share God's Gifts
150: t. Icon courtesy St. Nektarios Church, Boston, MA; b. Icon courtesy Dormition Church, Somerville, MA.
151: Icon courtesy Dormition Church, Somerville, MA.

Christmas
152: Icon courtesy St. Nektarios Church, Boston, MA.
Sunday of Orthodoxy
154: Areti Bratsis.
Easter
158: Icon courtesy St. Nektarios Church, Boston, MA.
Ascension
160: Icon courtesy Dormition Church, Somerville, MA.
Pentecost
162: Icon courtesy Dormition Church, Somerville, MA.